Do Something
in Your
Family

Amanda Rondeau

Consulting Editor, Diane Craig, M.A./Reading Specialist

Published by ABDO Publishing Company, 4940 Viking Drive, Edina, Minnesota 55435.

Copyright © 2004 by Abdo Consulting Group, Inc. International copyrights reserved in all countries. No part of this book may be reproduced in any form without written permission from the publisher. SandCastle™ is a trademark and logo of ABDO Publishing Company.

Printed in the United States.

Credits
Edited by: Pam Price
Curriculum Coordinator: Nancy Tuminelly
Cover and Interior Design and Production: Mighty Media
Photo Credits: BananaStock Ltd., Corbis Images, Comstock, Digital Vision, Image Source, Rubberball Productions

Library of Congress Cataloging-in-Publication Data

Rondeau, Amanda, 1974-.
    Do something in your family / Amanda Rondeau.
        p. cm.--(Do something about it!)
    Includes index.
    ISBN 1-59197-574-3
    1. Child volunteers--Juvenile literature. 2. Social action--Juvenile literature. 3. Community development--Juvenile literature. 4. Quality of life--Juvenile literature. I. Title. II. Series.

    HQ784.V64 R663 2004
    361--dc21

                                                                    2003058391

SandCastle™ books are created by a professional team of educators, reading specialists, and content developers around five essential components that include phonemic awareness, phonics, vocabulary, text comprehension, and fluency. All books are written, reviewed, and leveled for guided reading, early intervention reading, and Accelerated Reader® programs and designed for use in shared, guided, and independent reading and writing activities to support a balanced approach to literacy instruction.

Let Us Know

After reading the book, SandCastle would like you to tell us your stories about reading. What is your favorite page? Was there something hard that you needed help with? Share the ups and downs of learning to read. We want to hear from you! To get posted on the ABDO Publishing Company Web site, send us e-mail at:

sandcastle@abdopub.com

SandCastle Level: Transitional

You can make a difference in your family by doing something to make your home a better place to live.

When you do something to help others, you are making a difference.

Ms. Smith wants her daughter to know what she does at work.

Sometimes she brings Talia to the office.

The Garcias want to eat healthy meals.

They make healthy food together every night.

The Veron family thinks recycling is important.

Mr. Veron sorts his family's recyclables.

Mrs. Ullman wants Nora
to have healthy habits.

She teaches Nora to
brush her teeth every
morning.

Kelly's family likes to be in their backyard.

Kelly helps her dad take care of the flower garden.

Liz's grandma lives far away.

Liz calls her grandma every week so they can stay close.

Rose knows her little sister can't do everything older kids can do.

Rose tries to do things with her friends that Sophie can do too.

Jon knows his mom is busy.

He helps her with chores.

There are many ways you can make a difference in your family.

What would you like to do?

Glossary

backyard. the area behind a house

chore. a regular job or task, like cleaning your room

family. a group of people related to one another

flower. the part of a plant that makes the fruit or seed

garden. a place where flowers, vegetables, or other plants are grown

grandma. grandmother, the mother of your mother or father

habit. a behavior done so often that it becomes automatic

healthy. preserving the wellness of body, mind, or spirit; free from disease

meal. the portion of food eaten at breakfast, lunch, or dinner

office. a room or building where work is done, often at a desk

recyclable. an item such as a bottle or can that can be processed to create new items

tooth. plural, teeth; one of the white, bony parts of your mouth that you use to bite and chew

week. a period of seven days

About SandCastle™

A professional team of educators, reading specialists, and content developers created the SandCastle™ series to support young readers as they develop reading skills and strategies and increase their general knowledge. The SandCastle™ series has four levels that correspond to early literacy development in young children. The levels are provided to help teachers and parents select the appropriate books for young readers.

Emerging Readers
(no flags)

Beginning Readers
(1 flag)

Transitional Readers
(2 flags)

Fluent Readers
(3 flags)

These levels are meant only as a guide. All levels are subject to change.

ABDO
Publishing Company

To see a complete list of SandCastle™ books and other nonfiction titles from ABDO Publishing Company, visit **www.abdopub.com** or contact us at:

4940 Viking Drive, Edina, Minnesota 55435 • 1-800-800-1312 • fax: 1-952-831-1632